"Hot Potato is a problem so controversial and sensitive that it is risky to deal with. For example, gun control is a political hot potato. This term, dating from the mid-1800s, alludes to the only slightly older expression "drop like a hot potato," meaning "to abandon something or someone quickly" (lest one be burned.) The idiom alludes to the fact that cooked potatoes retain considerable heat because they contain a lot of water."

The American Heritage Idioms Dictionary
Houghton Mifflin Company, 2002

Imagined, yet potato-plausible headlines.

Alien and Sedition Hot Potatoes Decide 1800 Election

Embargo Hottest Potato of 1807 for Jefferson

Polk's Oregon Border Hot Potato

Buchanan Tosses Secession
Hot Potato to Lincoln

Zimmerman Telegram Hot Potato
May Force Wilson into War

FDR's Court Packing Hot Potato

Truman's Hottest Potato Decisions
Dropping the Bomb & Firing Mac

Will JFK Drop Cuban Hot Potato?

Can Carter Handle
Hostage Hot Potato?

Health Care & Immigration
Hot Potatoes Dropped Again

"Hot Potato" Capital of the World

DC Nickname Campaign

by Tom Hughes

EATS Publishing
Albuquerque, New Mexico

Dedicated to Gulliver.

In memory of
Jack Hill,
Ann & John Niederhauser

Thanks especially to Meredith and
my students at the International School of Brussels in the
1970s who helped me create
The Potato Museum.

Contents

New York?	The Big Apple
Boston?	Beantown
Chicago?	The Windy City
Los Angeles?	The Big Orange
Honolulu?	The Big Pineapple
New Orleans?	The Big Easy

Washington, DC ?????????????

Every city has a moniker, a nickname to call its own, but there is none for our nation's capital.

DC Nickname Campaign nominates:
"Washington DC: The Hot Potato!"

Perfect, right?

No city on earth has juggled (tossed, dropped or passed) as many hot potato issues as good old "no taxation without representation" District of Columbia.

Hot Potato: n. inf. A controversial issue or situation that is awkward or unpleasant to deal with.
---*Oxford Current English Dictionary*, 2009

WDC: where devilishly difficult-to-resolve issues are tackled, or not, every day by all branches of government, executive, judicial and congressional.

This book is about my long-standing belief that Washington, DC is indeed "The Hot Potato." A nickname it has earned. An association with the noble tuber that is fitting and complimentary. After all, potatoes are significantly more valuable and versatile a commodity than apples any day. And potatoes are all-American in origin. Apples come from Kazakhstan. Apple pie is not really American, but any way you prepare them, potatoes are. Better to be identified with the world's number one vegetable than a fruit saddled with this saying: "It takes only one to spoil the barrel."

Thirty years ago, my wife and I opened the world's first museum dedicated to potatoes in a gallery space of our Capitol Hill townhouse. Here's part of a New York Times article from that time. "Mr. Hughes, who says the potato provides more food value per acre than rice or wheat, quotes approvingly from *Hymn to the Potato*, by the Brooklyn poet Menke Katz: *On the hungry alleys of my childhood, the milky way was a potato land.*

"Asked why the potato museum is in Washington, Mr. Hughes explained that "it should be in the city where every day people are handling hot potatoes. Can you think of a city that handles more ?"He said he had urged Mayor Marion S. Barry to get Washington formally called the Hot Potato, as New York is called the Big Apple. 'I'm getting a little tired hearing all that Big Apple bit,' he said. 'The potato is a hell of a lot more nutritious and more versatile and economically more important than apples ever will be.'" http:// www.nytimes.com/1985/08/28/us/one-potato-two-potato.html

So sure, New York is the HQ for the UN. Yes, they take up a lot of "pomme de terres chauds and "patatas calientes." But do they really resolve any thorny world issues or just toss them around before dropping them altogether?

But DC, especially on the president's desk, in the halls of Congress and at the Supreme Court's bench, is where the hottest potatoes of all land. If they could be handled by others they would.

Over the years, hot potatoes pertaining to wars, rights and financial affairs have been ever-present issues making headlines in Washington. Others, such as civil service reform and tariffs (high, low or abolished,) have been potatoes so fiery to handle that they were passed on through a series of administrations during the nation's "gilded age." Many were one time affairs. Here's a brief list. Can you match the "hot potato" with the president in office at the time?

Affordable Health Care, gun control, War on Terror, Terri Schiavo, stem cell, Equal Rights Amendment, immigration reform, energy policy, "Too Big to Fail," "Don't Ask, Don't Tell," NAFTA, Guantanamo, Iran Nuclear Talks, Star Wars Defense Systems, Iran Hostage Crisis, Civil Rights Act, Cuban Missile Crisis, McCarthyism, public school integration, Berlin Airlift, Taft-Hartley Act, General MacArthur dismissal, Japanese internment, packing Supreme Court, New Deal, Bonus Army, Prohibition, Farm Price Supports, teaching evolution, Teapot Dome, women's suffrage, League of Nations, child labor, federal income tax, United Mine Workers strike, FDA, Philippine independence, Sherman Anti-Trust, Oriental Exclusion Act, Reconstruction, railroad strikes, Emancipation, the draft, annexation of Hawaii, Fugitive Slave Act, Mexican-American War, Vice-Presidential succession, Indian relocation, women's labor unions, freedom of the seas, Louisiana Purchase, abolition, Alien and Sedition Acts, tax rebellions.

Still a Hot Potato

Official prayers for Obama are a political hot potato

Look out! Keystone XL Pipeline Project Hot Potato Incoming

Republicans are playing hot potato with Homeland Security funding

Dropping a Client Like a "Hot Potato"

U.S. Supreme Court Passes the Buck on Affirmative Action Hot Potato

Obama and Congress Play Hot Potato With War Powers in Syria

High Court Ducks Hot Potato Case

Senate tosses shutdown hot potato back to House

HOT POTATO BENGHAZI

Part 1

Hot Potatoes Dominate Washington Headlines

Headlines demonstrate that WDC is linked to potatoes, now and forever. So why not give in to the obvious? Washington, DC is the "Hot Potato Capital of the World," or just simply "The Hot Potato."

I'm not even talking about the fact that Washington is often miserably hot in the summer. Average temperatures in the humid high 80s attest to that. The city was built in a swamp, after all. Another of the many unfavorable monikers DC has been tagged with over the years is "Swamplandia."

WDC: The City of Derogatory, Lame, and Downright Embarrassing Nicknames

No nickname ever has adhered successfully to the city. No surprise, as political Washington, as opposed to the actual city, doesn't have a positive reputation or image. Here's a list of DC's mostly unflattering nicknames and slogans.

District of Corruption
Hollywood for Ugly People
Fat Cat City
City of Acronyms
Alphabet City
The Big Lanyard
Gridlock Town
Murder Capital of America (late 1980s to early 1990s)
One City
City of Words
City Beautiful (also used to designate Miami)
51st State Wannabe
Cap City
Chocolate City (other cities so nicknamed)
Where Class Presidents Go to Die
Bullshit City (trucker term)
A Work-Free Drug Place (a WaPost's "Invite" entry)

"Overeducated, Underrepresented" is a cute, but partly inaccurate takeoff on the DC license tagline "Taxation without Representation," as the District's public schools struggle with high dropout rates.

"City of Magnificent Distances" is the nickname preferred by a popular DC neighborhood blogger who posed the question some years back: "Does DC need a nickname?" Yes, was the response. "The Hot Potato" was not mentioned. By the way, "City of Magnificent Distances" seems more appropriate for spread-out cities like Jacksonville or Houston, not DC which measures a mere ten miles across. The "City of Magnificent Distances" nickname was first mentioned in a 1881 Grand Traverse (MI) Herald supplement. http://www.popville.com/?s=DC+nickname&submit=Search

"DMV," for District/Maryland/Virginia, is in limited use around the greater DC metro area mostly by headline writers but, for many, DMV stands for the often disliked Department of Motor Vehicles.

Importance of Nicknames

"Washington, D.C., the capital of the United States of America, has been known by a variety of nicknames, aliases, sobriquets and slogans, both officially and unofficially, now and in the past."

The American Rome
The Capital of the World
City of Magnificent Intentions (coined by Charles Dickens)
The Federal City
Nation's Capital
A Capital City

"City nicknames can help in establishing a civic identity, helping outsiders recognize a community or attracting people to a community because of its nickname; promoting civic pride; and building community unity. Nicknames and slogans that successfully create a new community "ideology or myth" are also believed to have economic value. Their economic value is difficult to measure, but there are anecdotal reports of cities that have achieved substantial economic benefits by "branding" themselves by adopting new slogans."
(http://en.wikipedia.org/wiki/Nicknames_of_Washington,_D.C.)

Wanted: Nickname for WDC

Perhaps WDC's importance explains the lack of a subtitle. It simply doesn't need one. NYC may be a global financial hub and home of the UN. But Washington doesn't have the luxury of falling back on Wall Street's "too big to fail" line or dropping the hot potatoes the UN is handed. And the UN doesn't really "govern" anything. Washington does. WDC, not always, but certainly for the last century, has been one of the main centers of power in the world.

WDC may qualify as the one place beyond needing a moniker or motto, but that doesn't prevent a legion of PR types, tourism touts, promoters, image builders, editors, journalists, headline composers, song writers, novelists and me from thinking it needs one. We've got a point. Who wants to keep writing, reading or hearing "Washington-this" and "Washington-that" endlessly? The time for a catchy nickname is long past due.

The city has ventured into this nickname game from time to time as well. But the results were so uninspiring, little can be found about them on the web, except for former Mayor Grey's "One City."

Which leads us to the purpose of this book and the nickname campaign it is spearheading. Here's an April 2015 screenshot of what comes from a Google search of "Washington DC: The Hot Potato." I hope the DC Nickname Campaign will yield different results soon.

Web   Images   Shopping   News   Videos   More ▾   Search tools

About 1,530,000 results (0.42 seconds)

Hot Potato Cafe - CLOSED - American (New) - Washington ...
www.yelp.com › Restaurants › American (New) ▾ Yelp ▾
★★★✭☆ Rating: 3.5 - 35 reviews - Price range: $
Hot Potato Cafe - Artichoke-poblano mix - Washington, DC, United States Hot Potato
Cafe - spinach, feta and roasted garlic potatoe - Washington, DC, Hot ...

Hot Potato Cafe 614 E St NW Washington | Order Delivery ...
https://www.grubhub.com/washington-dc/hot-potato-cafe-... ▾ GrubHub.com ▾
Order delivery online from Hot Potato Cafe in Washington instantly! View Hot Potato
Cafe's May 2015 deals, coupons & menus. Order delivery online right now or by phone
... 614 E St NW Washington, DC. Friday. Not taking orders at this time.

Potato Museum - Wikipedia, the free encyclopedia
en.wikipedia.org/wiki/Potato_Museum ▾ Wikipedia ▾
For other Potato Museums, see List of Potato Museums. ... The museum was based in
Washington, DC for several years and open by appointment only.
You've visited this page 5 times. Last visit: 5/5/15

Hot Potato: How Washington and New York Gave Birth to ...
www.amazon.com › ... › African-American Studies ▾ Amazon.com, Inc. ▾
Hot Potato: How Washington and New York Gave Birth to Black Basketball and ...
When Edwin Henderson introduced the game to Washington, D.C., in 1907, ...

Hot Potato Cafe - Washington, DC | Groupon
www.groupon.com › ... › Food & Drink › Restaurants ▾ Groupon ▾
Hot Potato serves up tantalizing tubers artfully festooned with an assemblage of
imaginative toppings, such as pulled pork, chicken, avocado, and fresh ...

WDC and The Potato:
Pairing The Planet's Most Powerful City and Plant

But first, in case you think it's a little bit inappropriate to be linking the de-facto capital of the world to the potato, let's briefly examine the history and social influence of the tuber. Identifying Washington, DC with the potato is a no-brainer, once you know the facts about the tremendous tater.

There is no species of human food that can be consumed in a greater variety of modes than the potato.
--James Sinclair

Potatoes are the world's number one vegetable and easily one of the most valuable plants on the planet. They have eliminated chronic malnutrition wherever they've been cultivated; made possible the vast Incan empire; played a huge role in the Industrial Revolution, precipitated the fall of Communism, allowed communities to become established in previously uninhabitable high mountain valleys in the American Rockies, Europe's Alps and Asia's Himalayas. (Many of Nepal's earthquake-destroyed villages were there because of the potato.) Elsewhere, persistent reliance on a single potato variety and other reckless policies caused crop failure, famine and mass migration from Ireland to the USA where the hardworking Irish helped build America. There are over 7,000 varieties in the world, thousands of recipes and hundreds of industrial uses.

Spuds have inspired songwriters, filmmakers, writers and artists. Two of the most recognized paintings in the world have potato themes: Van Gogh's "The Potato Eaters" and Millet's "Angelus" (the French couple giving thanks over their potato harvest.) Potato starch crystals made possible the world's first color photographs known as autochromes.

"Seeing the beauty of a potato field in bloom for the first time surprises many people. Its flowers--clean white, blush pink, soft violet, even a deep blue. And its simple parallel lines, green alternating with color. Agricultural landscapes hold their own with any other. The potato itself is unique among plants for its quiet influence on the world's history and culture. From its origins in the Andes mountains, the potato has traveled farther than any vegetable, around the globe and to the outskirts of the Moon. It has inserted deep roots in places where people think it has always been. That's why many call it the *Irish spud*, or the *Idaho potato*."
---Meredith Hughes, potatomuseum.com

"In the space of just 400 years, the potato has become a staple crop of many people around the world whose antecedents had subsisted perfectly well upon grain crops for anything up to 4000 years. The reason for this somewhat surprising development is that the potato is the best all-around bundle of nutrition known to mankind.

"Its ration of carbohydrate to protein is such that anyone eating enough potatoes to satisfy their energy requirements will automatically obtain most of the protein they require. Furthermore, the "biological value" of potato protein (an index of the nitrogen absorbed from a food and retained by the body for growth and maintenance) is 73, second only to eggs at 96; just ahead of soybeans at 72, but far superior to corn (maize) at 54 and wheat at 53.

"Potatoes also contain significant amounts of essential vitamins (the British, in fact, used to derive 30% of their vitamin C intake from potatoes.) Exceptional productivity is another virtue of the potato. A field of potatoes produces more energy per hectare per day than a field of any other crop. Potatoes grow well from sea level to 14,000 feet on a wider variety of soils, under a wider range of climatic conditions, than any other staple food. The potato matures faster in 90 to 120 days, and will provide small but edible tubers in just 60 days.

"All in all, the potato is about the world's most efficient means of converting plant, land, water and labour into a palatable and nutritious food. --John Reader, *Man on Earth*, 1998." (See also Reader's *Potato, A History of the Propitious Esculent* which was published in 2009.)

Washington, DC: Full of Potatoes

Beyond the importance of the potato plant, which nobody can deny, is the fact that the nation's capital has long been full of them. DC straddles the Potomac to include a slice of Virginia, the colony where at Jamestown in 1619 potatoes were first grown and consumed. Potatoes have been a staple crop since what was to become Washington was nothing more than some isolated farms and the small riverside port of Georgetown. Washingtonians always have been potato eaters. From the earliest days as the nation's capital, every resident from the humblest rooming house dweller to the first families and diplomats ate spuds. Bowls of steaming boiled potatoes were served in elaborately decorated silver rings, by the latter, in order to protect their highly polished dining table surfaces from the hot potatoes.

During two world wars, public spaces and front yards including the White House grounds were planted in Victory Gardens, and all included potatoes. During WWII, Vice President Henry Wallace supposedly planted a potato patch in his DC front yard, drawing criticism from an indignant neighbor.

Americans always have consumed at least four times more potatoes than any other vegetable. In Washington, as elsewhere, the spud is consumed in greater variety than most other food plants. Consumption of vodka, schnapps, aquavit and even beer made from potatoes lifts the spirits of many, including politicians and their lobbyists.

The nation's founding fathers and many of its subsequent chief executives were potato farmers, for example Grant and Truman. Potatoes have shaped policy decisions, too. The Wilson administration, for instance, had to cope with a prolonged World War I because the German army was so well supplied with potatoes. The British people, meanwhile, were asked to forgo potatoes on certain days, so the nation's output could be sent to the troops in the frontline trenches. American cargo ships braved German blockades of British ports to deliver much needed food relief.

Punch Magazine cartoon, 1917 (author's collection)

The FDR administration had to plan for the impact of German potato alcohol-fueled rockets attacking British cities and endangering U.S. interests. The Truman administration dealt with a glut of potatoes that led to protests and price instabilities. Cold War politics also created some bizarre tater -related incidents. An unusual court martial occurred when a DC area soldier was exonerated of having "destroyed government property" while on KP. He had been accused of peeling potatoes too thickly. (New York Times, June, 19, 1959)

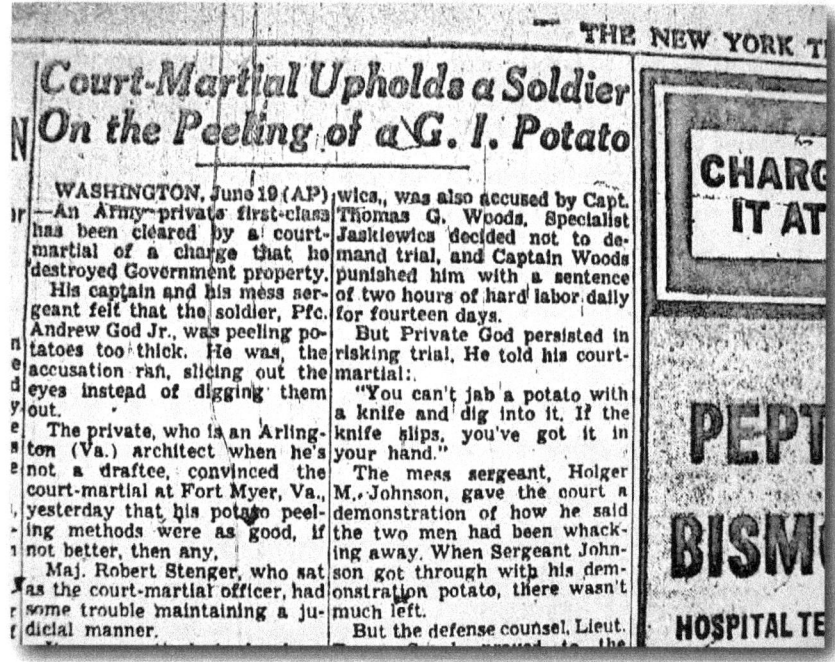

More seriously, military and security agencies had to handle accusations that the U.S. government was using biological warfare by dropping potato bugs on East German potato fields in an attempt to damage their vital food supply.

In recent decades taters have taken center stage in Washington politics. Vice-President Dan Quayle's gaff of misspelling potato with an 'e' is still remembered.

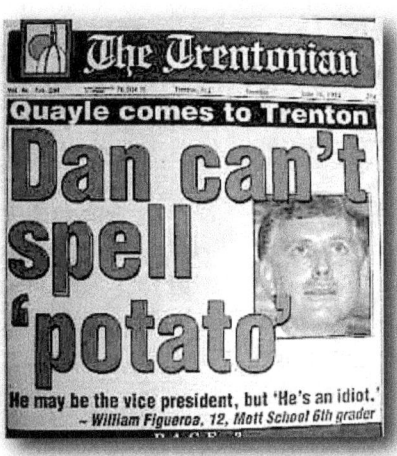

President Reagan declared ketchup, French fries' constant condiment companion, a vegetable. Serving "Freedom Fries" rather than "French fries" in the Congressional cafeterias was a much publicized rebuke to the French by a couple of Congressmen, as France did not join the Gulf War coalition. And then there was the USDA school lunch guidelines flap which sought to restrict the serving of potatoes to only once a week. This leads to the perennial hot potato over whether potatoes are a prime factor in the nation's obesity crisis. Now revised federal guidelines emanating from Washington have downplayed that concern. Many claim that sugar is the real culprit.

Potatoes are a complex carbohydrate, as opposed to carbs derived from sugarcane. Too many carbs, simple or complex, are what make us fat. Yes, it's complicated, and another "hot potato." So the best advice is to eat everything in moderation and get plenty of exercise. Fitness fans President Obama and First Lady Michelle are fond of potatoes, also.

Hail to the Red Skinneds!   Spuds on the Warpath

According to the The Washington Post, the city's NFL team "hot potato" name has had an easy remedy for decades. "People have been making the same Redskins potato suggestion for (at least) 27 years." (http://www.washingtonpost.com/blogs/dc-sports-bog/wp/2014/06/19/people-have-been-making-the-same-redskins-potato-suggestion-for-at-least-27-years/)

"The least disruptive and most cost-effective solution for the Skins would be to replace the formidable proud American Indian profile with the humble redskin potato. That should shut the libs up until they realize that potatoes are members of the tobacco family."   http://daletoons.blogspot.com/2014/06/in-recent-years-closest-thing-team-has.html

Do-It-Yourself Redskin Helmet Conversion Project

1. Grow red potatoes.
2. Harvest some.
3. Wash one.
4. Dry.
5. Cut it in half.
6. Dip cut side in red paint.
7. Press potato onto slippery sides of white helmet.
8. Fail miserably.
9. Abandon project.
10. Toast the Red Skins---team or taters---with a shot of potato vodka.

Note: many potato varieties reference American Indians. Among them: Adirondack Red, Chieftain, Red Pontiac, Red Cloud, Caribe and Katahdin.

WDC and the World's First Potato Museum

Washington, DC was the home of the world's first, and for a time, only museum about the potato. It still is, according to this popular Denver International Airport art installation: "America: Why I Love Her" by Gary Sweeney, 1994)

Note:
"Potato Museum,
Washington"
is the only site listed for our
nation's capital at Denver
International Airport's
"America: Why I Love Her"
art map.

The Potato Museum...that idiosyncratic and deadly serious institution.---NY Times

The Potato Museum is of the new modern type, which cuts across academic frontiers; it's an enthusiast's museum and our hard, cold, cynical world desperately needs enthusiasm.
---Kenneth Hudson, author of Museums of Influence

....a museum that gives sustenance the kind of attention museums give to wars, airplanes, human tragedy and the like.
---Christian Science Monitor

The most important issue confronting the human race is how we are going to preserve the quality of the environment and still feed the rapidly growing population into the next millennium. The Potato Museum provides a vehicle to get the message across.
---Dr. John Niederhauser, World Food Prize winner, 1990

Remembering *The Potato Museum*
by Rachel Adams "The Capitol Hill Current" 12/08/05

"Perhaps the oddest little-known fact about the Capitol Hill neighborhood during the mid-1980's and early 1990's, the world's first museum devoted exclusively to potatoes resided within it, housed in a simple town home on North Carolina Avenue, SE. The original impetus for the museum, which Meredith and Tom Hughes operated in their Capitol Hill home from 1985 to 1993, was Thomas Hughes' stint as an elementary teacher in Brussels, Belgium during the mid 1970s. While living and working there, Hughes noticed the prevalence of the potato in the city; many families kept gardens, devoted solely to potato-growing, a hold-over from the days when Belgians had to largely feed themselves as their country was repeatedly invaded and fought over. Hughes asked the 10 year old students in his class to do a project on this phenomenon, with surprising results---the amount of material gathered by the students about the significance of the potato was quite vast, and the assignment morphed into a semi-permanent, three room school exhibit, maintained for three years and covered extensively by the European press. When Hughes relocated to Washington in 1983, he brought the interest and his ever growing collection with him. Two years later, he and his wife opened the by-appointment-only gallery on the ground floor of their house.

"The Potato Museum was almost instantly embraced by Washingtonians, tourists and the local press, its displays ranging from the historical to the avant-garde to the downright strange. One exhibit presented information about the early cultivation in South America; another discussed the Irish potato famine of the mid-19th century; another explored the presence of the potato in recent film and music (explaining, for instance, the "mashed potato" dance of the 1950's.) Visitors marveled at the first potato-powered clock, Art Deco-inspired potato mashers from the 1920's, a bottle of potato vodka, strangely shaped potatoes sent to the museum from around the country, a well-preserved pair of 4,000 year old tubers found during a Peruvian archaeological dig and more than 300 objects from all continents and three dozen nations. The site of the former Potato Museum in Capitol Hill is now, again, a privately owned home. But it remains, in the minds of those Washingtonians who still remember it, an art-space equally as valid as and perhaps more whimsical than any of those grand Smithsonians downtown."

The Potato Museum on North Carolina Avenue hosted all - potato feasts, once a month, one attended by Washington Post restaurant critic Phyllis Richman. Two couples had their first date there and another got engaged. The co-founders of the International Potato Center, Dr. Richard Sawyer and Dr. John Niederhauser, attended meetings there. It was a key location for a Japanese TV crew filming a documentary about the potato chip. The Smithsonian's Herman Viola toured the exhibit and hired us to join his team of guest curators for the National Museum of Natural History's epic "Seeds of Change" exhibit for the quincentenary of the Columbian Exchange. Along with the State Department's Reception Rooms and Alexandria's Old Tavern it was the site for Colonial Williamsburg's docent training field trips. And when the museum closed, it was the subject of a Washington Post editorial.

The Museum of Second Helpings
Washington Post editorial November 24, 1989

"You probably don't feel like eating anything more just yet. You may even be thinking right now that this year it won't be all that difficult to accomplish your annually promised six-month-long abstention from food. But when you change your mind about this, as you surely will, one possible fallback is to take yourself out of the house and head down to Capitol Hill for a couple of hours in the world's only Museum of the Potato."

The Washington Post

FRIDAY, NOVEMBER 24, 1989

The Museum of Second Helpings

YOU PROBABLY don't feel like eating anything more just yet. You may even be thinking right now that this year it won't be all that difficult to accomplish your annually promised six-month-long abstention from food. But when you change your mind about this, as you surely will, one possible fallback is to take yourself out of the house and head down to Capitol Hill for a couple of hours in the world's only Museum of the Potato. The New York Times recently reported that this little-known family-run museum, which offers more than 2,000 exhibits on the history, nutrition, aesthetics and cultural impact of the potato, is being seriously wooed by no fewer than six states that want to transplant it to their own turf and make it a tourist attraction. If you've stayed unaware of the Potato Museum for the four years it's been quietly ripening in Washington, this may be your last chance to gaze on the exhibits and nurse dreamy memories of Thursday's yams.

Except that co-owner Meredith Hughes will scold you if you do, for assuming that yams or sweet potatoes have any relationship whatsoever to the classic potato, or spud. This, Mrs. Hughes says, is one of the leading misconceptions about potatoes—that they are at all related to yams, a tropical vegetable, or to sweet potatoes, a distant relative of the morning glory. Potatoes, though, have their own legitimate claim to a place at Thanksgiving: like corn they are a New World vegetable, cultivated for millennia in the Andes and brought back by the Spaniards to Spain in the 1600s. After this they played a steadily more important role in poor laborers' diets, most famously in Ireland till the potato famine, and are even credited by a theorist or two (so says the admittedly partisan Mrs. Hughes) with helping make the Industrial Revolution feasible.

Other potato distinctions that the museum features and that have helped it to draw the interested attention of tourism-development types in Maine, Idaho, Colorado, North Dakota, Washington and Wisconsin: that the potato is the fourth-largest staple food on earth, after wheat, rice and corn; that it is grown in the Arctic Circle and in the Israeli deserts; and that the Mr. Potato Head doll by Hasbro was the first toy ever advertised on television. Oh, and that Mrs. Hughes, who with her teacher husband, Thomas, founded the endeavor in 1983, has been arguing almost since then that "Washington: A Hot Potato" would be a great motto for this city once it gets tired of that "capital" joke, and that Washington is the logical place for this museum to stay. The Hugheses feel that people in an urban, non-potato-growing area need their museum more than residents of potato-staple farming states like Maine or Idaho or the rest—and they are hopeful about an expression of interest they recently received from the Agricultural Research Station in Beltsville. Meanwhile, they're open by appointment, 544-1558.

Some of The Potato Museum's collection on display at the U.S. Botanic Garden in 2010.

The Hottest Potatoes in U.S. Political History

Clearly the links long have been forged between the powerful potato and the power center of the planet. Still need a little convincing that DC is "The Hot Potato" Capital of the World? Take a look at this list of just a few of the overheated issues tossed back and forth between the executive and legislative branches throughout the nation's history.

44 Obama

Human trafficking/abortion/Attorney General nomination; police brutality; Benghazi/Libya; IRS; Secret Service snafus; Affordable Care Act; Immigration Reform; gun sale background checks; War Powers Act; Syria; ISIS; Iran nuclear deal; BP Gulf oil spill; net neutrality

43 GW Bush

9/11; Patriot Act; war on terror; Afghan and Iraq Wars; failed hunt for Bin Laden; Homeland Security; FEMA's Katrina response; Terry Schiavo; stem cell debate; Kyoto; drilling in Alaska arctic; Guantanamo; Enron; immigration reform and border fence; assault weapons ban renewal

42 Clinton

NAFTA; Bosnia War; cloning; health care reform; Brady Bill; government shutdown; Welfare to Work; Whitewater; Haiti's Aristide; gun show sales; Lewinsky affair; impeachment; budget surplus; Rwanda genocide response

41 GHW Bush

Secretary of Treasury tax evasion; S & L Bailout; Exxon Valdez oil spill; Air Act of 1970 (emissions limit debate); "no new taxes" pledge; Rodney King riots; overthrow of Panama's Noriega; Persian Gulf crisis; Start 1 Treaty; NAFTA; Somalia; Supreme Court nominations; Anita Hill v Clarence Thomas;

40 Reagan

Iran-Contra Affair; trickle-down economics; federal budget expansion; Interior Secretary Watts' pro exploitation policies; jet sales to Saudi Arabia; Marine peacekeeping in Lebanon; Beirut Marine Barracks attack; Nicaraguan and El Salvador civil wars; Granada invasion; Star Wars Defense System; air traffic controllers' strike

39 Carter

Draft evaders pardon; DOE; Cruise missiles replacing B-1 bomber; Soviet invasion of Afghanistan; boycott of Moscow Olympic games; Camp David Accords; Education Department creation; inflation from 6% to 15%; human rights campaign; Salt II Treaty; Shah of Iran; Iran Hostages Crisis; failed attempt to rescue hostages

38 Ford

Inflation; Turkish invasion of Cyprus; amnesty program for draft evaders; high unemployment; fall of Saigon; Mayaguez Affair

37 Nixon

Vietnam War; China visit; wage and price controls to fight inflation; 26th amendment, voting age 18; draft, lottery, all - volunteer army; ABM "Safeguard" treaty; school busing to comply with court '69 ruling; Supreme Court nominees' fights; women's Equal Rights Amendment; EPA creation; gas shortages of '73; War Powers Resolution; Watergate coverup/ tapes; Watergate investigator Cox firing

36 Johnson

Medicare 1966; War on Poverty; civil rights marches; Civil Rights Bill 1964; railroad crisis, 15 day cooling off; Gulf of Tonkin Crisis (led to build-up in Vietnam, from 16,000 in '64 to 500,000 in '68);

Vietnam War lies (revealed in Pentagon papers); Republican opposition to Great Society Programs; race riots '67

35 Kennedy
Bay of Pigs '61; Cuban Missile Crisis '62; Atomic Test Ban Treaty; Berlin Wall; prayer in schools; Amendment 23 (DC vote); integration of Universities of Mississippi and Alabama; South Vietnamese government repression of Buddhists

34 Eisenhower
Gifts controversy; McCarthyism; communist aggression in Asia, Latin America, Africa; Spudnik; enforcing civil rights laws; amendment to limit presidential treaty-making powers; farm support reform; Atoms for Peace program; Korean War truce; public school integration; Sherman Adams resignation; Quemoy Islands crisis; U-2 Spy plane; break with Cuba

33 Truman
Firing of 166 IRS workers; atomic bombs dropped; Amendment 22 limiting presidential terms; Berlin airlift; Labor-Management Relations Act or Taft-Hartley Act over veto; Marshall Plan; Fair Employment Practices to protect minority rights; Korean Conflict; dismissal of General MacArthur; fears of communist infiltration of government

32 Roosevelt
Depression; New Deal; Bank Holiday; WPA; National Labor Relations Act; national debt; packing Supreme Court; Neutrality Acts of 1930s; Japanese internment; presidential term limits

31 Hoover
Bonus Army, handling of veterans seeking pay bonuses; Prohibition; stock market crash/depression; Federal Farm Board; Smoot-Hawley; Emergency Relief Act

30 Coolidge
Veto of WW I vets bonus bill; veto of farm price support bills; Muscle Shoals power plant; unregulated business speculation; World Court membership

29 Harding
Teapot Dome oil lease scandal; League of Nations deadlock; "return to normalcy;" Prohibition, 18th Amendment; teaching evolution in schools

28 Wilson
U.S. Navy scandal at Newport; women's suffrage; direct election of senators; Prohibition; Child Labor Act; Mexico-Tampico Affair; WW I neutrality; League of Nations; Wilson's health

27 Taft
Interior Secretary Ballinger's mines controversy; Women's Suffrage; Amendment 16: federal income tax; Payne-Aldrich Tariff: tariffs high

26 Roosevelt, T.
Panama Canal; FDA; trusts; United Mine Workers strike; Department of Commerce; Alaska-Canada boundary dispute; Hepburn Railway Act; San Francisco segregation of Japanese students

25 McKinley
Remember the Maine; Spanish-American War; Philippine independence movement; citizens' rights in colonial territories; anti-trust laws enforcement

24 Cleveland
Veteran's pensions; Pullman Strike of 1894; Hawaii annexation

23 Harrison, B
High tariffs and surplus; Sherman Anti-Trust Act of 1890; Reciprocal Trade Agreement; Oriental Exclusion Act of 1892

22 Cleveland
His illegitimate child: "Ma, Ma, where's my Pa?"; low interest loans for farmers; high tariff protection for manufacturers; gold standard debate; Indian policy

21 Arthur
Pendleton Civil Service Act; lower tariffs for consumers; Chinese immigration

20 Garfield
Post Office corruption over "star routes"; Civil Service reform

19 Hayes
Stolen election; Stanley Matthew's Supreme Court nomination; ending Reconstruction; Railroad Strike of 1877; Civil Service reform

18 Grant
Whiskey Ring; Amendment 15; Civil Service reform efforts "spoils system"; Black Friday gold speculation; proposed purchase of Dominican Republic; Greenback Party; Credit Mobilier controversy

17 Johnson, A
Radical Republicans refusal to seat elected southerners; Reconstruction policy; Tenure of Office Act; impeachment

16 Lincoln
Secession; Civil War policy; draft; Habeas Corpus suspended; Emancipation Proclamation

15 Buchanan
Dred Scott case/slavery; Missouri Compromise; Secession; John Brown case of 1859; Bleeding Kansas

14 Pierce
Ostend Manifesto: taking Cuba as slave state; Kansas-Nebraska Act; annexation of Hawaii

13 Fillmore
Compromise of 1850; suffrage movement; Fugitive Slave Act

12 Taylor
Land compensation scandal involving Secretary of War; opposition to compromise with slave states

11 Polk
Mexican-American War; "54-40 or fight" Oregon border dispute with Canada; child labor conditions; immigrant poverty

10 Tyler
Whig party decline; Vice-presidential succession; Texas annexation

9 Harrison, W
Caroline Affair; Webster-Ashburton Treaty of 1842

8 Van Buren
Panic and Depression of 1837; Aroostock War boundary dispute with Canada; Seminole War

7 Jackson
States rights issues; spoils system; kitchen cabinet; Cherokee removal

6 Adams, JQ
1824 election ; women's labor unions; Tariff of Abominations

5 Monroe
Missouri Compromise: Maine, Missouri; roads and canals construction; First Seminole War; Florida acquired from Spain; Era of Good Feelings; Monroe Doctrine

4 Madison
General James Wilkinson Affair; relations with Great Britain and France: respect for US ships; War of 1812

3 Jefferson
Burr plot to create independent nation in midwest; treason trial; Barbary pirates; Embargo Act of 1807; Louisiana Purchase; states' rights; right of executive privilege; abolition of slave trade

2 Adams, J
XYZ Affair; Alien and Sedition Acts; "millions for defense, but not one cent for tribute"; Fries Rebellion of 1799; readiness of new capital city, Washington, DC

1 Washington (for the record only, as this administration was based in NYC and later Philadelphia) Jay Treaty: relations with GB; presidential protocol; Whiskey Rebellion

Hot Potatoes for the Courts, Agencies and Local Government

So there you have it. Many serious spuds sailed between the presidents and their Congressional sparring partners. But what about the many hot potatoes handled, or dropped, by the judiciary, DC city government, media and various organizations calling DC home?

The U.S. Supreme Court and other WDC based judicial bodies are, by definition, where controversial, contentious issues are considered. Historic hot potatoes handled or dropped by the top court include: campaign finance with Citizens United case, the Florida recount decision in Gore v Bush, abortion rights in Roe v Wade, school prayer. The list is long.

Every U.S. government agency has to deal with hot potatoes, as well. The U.S. State Department was tossed the Keystone XL Pipeline "hot potato" because it was an international matter involving Canada. The Interior Department has its endangered species preservation (think spotted owl) vs. development "hot potatoes." How about an emerging "hot potato" for the Treasury Department on how it will handle the growing pressure to have women pictured on US currency notes?

Next there are the super heated spuds at the local level. These involve streetcars, marijuana, funding family planning services, home rule vs. statehood, even the name of the city's professional football team. Of course we agree with those who have suggested settling the Redskins hot potato by keeping the name but re-imaging it as a red-skinned spud.

Other DC hot potatoes include whether to have Walmart stores, building height limits, restrictions on National Mall events and development vs. open space preservation.

Hot Potatoes for Individuals, Groups and Communities

Not just in "The Hot Potato" but everywhere, people face personal, family, group and community hot topics that they may wish to avoid out of fear of mishandling or dropping them altogether.

Personal hot potatoes include the many things people put off through procrastination: postponing going to the dentist or doctor over fear of the results; avoiding financial matters; suppressing thoughts that one may need to urgently explore, possibly with a professional.

Interpersonal "hot potatoes" between couples, for instance, include seemingly irreconcilable issues such as parenting styles, political or faith beliefs, housekeeping differences and resource allocations. These and other "hot potatoes" may lead to quiet, resentment-filled compromises rather than open discussions leading to workable solutions. Similar "hot potatoes" exist between family members, friends and neighbors.

Then there are the community and group "hot potatoes" that boil over in classrooms, workplaces, shops, restaurants and other public spaces. For instance, conflicts arise between often anonymous groups who, on the one hand, seek lower decibel levels in public spaces and those who feel that "noise" adds to the ambiance. (Some food writers are including decibel levels in their restaurant reviews.)

All manner of groups experience "hot potato" issues that prevent them from functioning efficiently. Here's some advice for employers on avoiding "hot potatoes" that can derail training sessions for employees.

"To tailor your program to the specific needs of your learners, interview two or three of your prospective learners to find out political "hot potatoes" and personal "hot button" issues that could arise in the classroom. Through pre-workshop interviews, one trainer discovered the group she was about to train had recently participated in a team building workshop that ended in conflict and disharmony, making their group interactions worse, not better. The group feared the upcoming workshop would be a repeat performance. Knowing this, the trainer was able to dispel the group's fears at the beginning of the workshop, and to set ground rules for a respectful, courteous classroom." *How to Train Employees: a guide for managers* by Bobette Hayes Williamson, 2007.
(http://www.amazon.com/How-Train-Employees-Managers-Edition-ebook/dp/B005IXQLES

"The hot potatoes game" is a term used to explain how graduate schools, but also other organizations, sometimes pass individuals with issues onto internships, expecting their problems will be addressed, but they aren't." (https://www.psychologytoday.com/blog/the-ethical-professor/201009/bad-apples-sometimes-become-hot-potatoes)

Part 2

DC Nickname Campaign: Take Action

For a variety of reasons, I hope you agree that DC is long overdue for a world-class nickname. One that will rival and exceed any other, including the gold standard of city appellations, New York's Big Apple. So, join us in making this happen.

GoPetition Sign and urge others to sign our on-line petition.
http://www.gopetition.com/petitions/dc-nickname-campaign-the-hot-potato.html

Activities
---Contact your local representatives and urge their support.
---Design different "DC: The Hot Potato" logos, artwork, cartoons, license plates and clothing.
---Create video, card and board games, banners, flags, apps.
---Compose a theme song or jingle, write a story or poem.
---Develop a public service ad, YouTube video.
---Produce something that goes viral.
Anything that helps the campaign.

Keep informed and contribute your ideas and actions to our online sites including:

Facebook: WDC: The Hot Potato
https://www.facebook.com/wdcthehotpotato?skip_nax_wizard=true&ref_type=logout_gear

Twitter:
https://twitter.com/WDCTheHotPotato

Tumblr: DC Nickname Campaign Blog
http://dcnicknamecampaign.tumblr.com/

Email: wdcthehotpotato@gmail.com

The Potato Museum Online: http://potatomuseum.com/

Cafe Press: Show your support for the campaign with "WDC: The Hot Potato" gear.

How will we track the campaign's success?
Google search hits for sure. There's nowhere to go but up. As of late April, searching "Washington DC: the hot potato" or any variation thereof produced no hits, zero. Also, the campaign's Twitter hashtags and other sites that track trends will provide more feedback.

All we need is you and your network. Thanks to social media and various internet tools, campaigns like this don't need huge budgets to pay for ad and public relations agencies, printed materials, mailings and such.

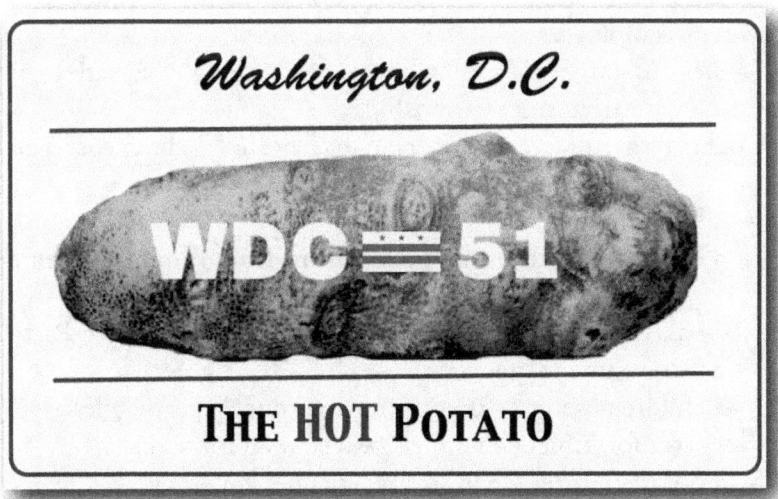

Hot Potato Facts, Fun, and Games

As a reward for your efforts, I invite you to play the various hot potato games and entertainments in the next section. But first get informed about all things hot potato. Soon you can impress, entertain and recruit your friends, family and others to join in this campaign. It's a "Hot Potato World," after all.

Hot Potato may refer to:
---a children's game that involves tossing a small object
---a high frequency trading effect
---an American TV game show in 1984
---a 1976 martial arts film with Jim Kelly
---a 2011 crime caper movie
---a La Toya Jackson song
---a popular video game
---another video game based on the 2008 Presidential election
---a routing strategy for computer networks
---an educational software suite
---a crop insurance incentive program
---a term for a high priority work task involving a sequence of employees
---an attractive person who passes through a series of unsuccessful relationships
---the term for when a person has been falsely accused of passing gas
---a live hand grenade
---a doctrine which prohibits law firms from dropping clients for more lucrative ones
---a baked potato and toppings fast food chain in Puerto Rico
---a video game maneuver
---a children's song by the Australian group "The Wiggles"
---a term for someone with excessive "swag" or vanity
---a phrase to utter when something goes your way
---in sports, passing a puck or ball around frantically or a pass that is difficult to handle

---some very unprintable sexual play and scatological activities
---a one-time restaurant in Philadelphia featured on "Gordon
     Ramsay's Kitchen Nightmares"
---a social media agency based in Brooklyn, NY
---an online food news and networking hub for Tompkins
     County, NY

<u>More About These Hot Potatoes</u>

"Hot potato volume effect" and "hot potato trading" are terms that describe what happens when high speed trading transactions pass back and forth "like hot potatoes." The same sales item, or currency, for instance, which causes wild fluctuations in the market price and other volatility issues. http://www.themoneyillusion.com/?p=23314

The "hot potato doctrine" means that law firms generally are prohibited from dropping smaller clients (like hot potatoes) in order to pick up more lucrative clients.
(http://law.marquette.edu/facultyblog/2009/03/25/hot-potato-conflicts/)

"The asylum seeker debate is the "Hot Potato" in Australian politics. Everyone's talking, no-one's listening. We aim to change that. That's why we created the hot potato van. And on the eve of the general election we took it on the road. Visiting 10 towns over 10 days, Busting 10 myths, Serving 10,000 potatoes, inspiring 10 million conversations. This is what happened." http://thehotpotato.com.au/

"The Hot Potato" (Papas Asadas) is a chain of fast food restaurants in Puerto Rico specializing in delicious Idaho baked potatoes with a variety of over 28 succulent toppings, salads, beverages, and desserts."http://www.thehotpotato.com/en/

"*Hot Potato* was a 1976 action film written and directed by Oscar Williams. The film was a Fred Weintraub and Paul

Heller production starring Jim Kelly. Jim Kelly also arranged his own fight scenes. *Hot Potato* was filmed on location in Chiang Mai, Thailand. It is a follow-up to Black Belt Jones. The film was distributed by Warner Bros. Pictures."
http://en.wikipedia.org/wiki/Hot_Potato_%28film%29

"*The Hot Potato* was a comedy crime thriller film from 2011. It was directed and written by Tim Lewiston and stars Ray Winstone, Colm Meaney and Jack Huston in the lead roles. This British film is a throwback to the crime caper films that were popular in the 1960s and pays homage to several of these, including *The Italian Job*."
http://en.wikipedia.org/wiki/The_Hot_Potato

"A shipment of potatoes headed from Germany to a Greek processing plant almost ended up arriving mashed, after a pair of World War II-era grenades were tucked into the taters before they hit the delivery truck. Workers on the washing line of the processing plant reported hearing odd sounds when the spuds hit the suds and when they checked, they found a pair of the vintage grenades swirling around in the mix. As it happened, the grenades were, in fact, still live: A bomb squad arrived to disarm them and send the potatoes on their way to hungry consumers." http://www.upi.com/Odd_News/2012/04/20/Germany-sends-grenades-in-potato-shipment/UPI-21201334966424/

Hot Potato Routing
"...in hot potato routing, each packet (of data) that is routed is constantly transferred until it reaches its final destination because the individual communication links cannot support more than one packet at a time. The packet is bounced around like a "hot potato," sometimes moving further away from its destination because it has to keep moving through the network. This technique allows multiple packets to reach their destinations without being dropped. This is in contrast

to "store and forward" routing where the network allows temporary storage at intermediate locations. Hot potato routing has applications in optical networks where messages made from light can not be stored in any medium." http://www.webopedia.com/TERM/H/hot_potato_routing.html

Air traffic control systems use hot potato routing. "Optical communication networks and air traffic management systems share the same fundamental routing problem as both optical packets and aircraft must continuously move within the network, while avoiding conflicts. We explore the use of hot potato and deflection routing algorithms, which are established routing methods in optical communication networks, in the conflict-free routing of air traffic. Hot potato algorithms allow the incorporation of conflict resolution constraints into the routing problem, in contrast to most approaches that decouple the optimal routing problem from the conflict resolution problem." http://ieeexplore.ieee.org/xpl/login.jsp?tp=&arnumber=1024904&url=http%3A%2F%2Fieeexplore.ieee.org%2Fxpls%2Fabs_all.jsp%3Farnumber%3D1024904

Sacred Cows and Hot Potatoes: Agrarian Myths in Agricultural Policy by William P. Browne, 1992

"The Hot Potatoes" educational software suite includes six applications, enabling you to create interactive multiple-choice, short-answer, jumbled-sentence, crossword, matching/ordering and gap-fill exercises for the World Wide Web." http://hotpot.uvic.ca/ "Hacking Hot Potatoes: The Cookbook is dedicated to extending the capabilities of a powerful suite of Web authoring tools - Hot Potatoes, by Half-Baked Software Inc. and the University of Victoria Humanities Computing and Media Centre. It is intended to help you make the best use of the Hot Potatoes suite so that you maximize the learning opportunities for your students. The recipes you will find in this book are both simple tricks and more complex code implementations to bring more interactivity into the exercises created with Hot Potatoes as well as using Hot Potatoes in Moodle." http://www.ewbooks.info/

Hot Potato Cafe was a restaurant in Philadelphia which appeared on season three of "Gordon Ramsay's Kitchen Nightmares" tv series. "Chef Gordon Ramsay visits Hot Potato Cafe, Philadelphia, PA to help three Sisters running a restaurant with their niece Danielle in the kitchen. The problems arose as they focused more on prettying up the restaurant and there was a bad review by a local newspaper in which the restaurant was dubbed as "Spuddy Hell". Danielle doesn't want to be a chef and is only there to help out the family. The owners don't seem to know what is wrong with the restaurant and upon seeing the menu he asks the sisters to recommend a dish each, no one recommends a potato dish to Gordon despite it being a potato themed restaurant. Gordon orders the Hot Potato Soup, Spud Skins and a Shepherds Pie, the Hot Potato Soup was "a mess" and "like lumps of glue", the three week old frozen Spud Skins tasted dreadful and the Shepherds Pie was "2/3 mash, 1/3 greasy minced lamb." http://www.kitchennightmaresblog.com/2011/05/us-season-3-episode-1-hot-potato-cafe.html#aGYWCC07qv452ugx.99

"Hot Potato" a social media agency based in Brooklyn, NY that provides event-based services acquired by Facebook in 2010. https://www.crunchbase.com/organization/hotpotato#sthash.zfGXWpFZ.dpuf

"Hot Potato Press" is the online food news and networking hub for Tompkins County, NY http://hotpotatopress.org/

"*Hot Potato* was a television game show broadcast on NBC in the United States from January 23 to June 29, 1984. Bill Cullen was the show's host. Two teams of three players, each sharing a common bond (e.g., occupation, mothers-to-be, etc.) competed. Cullen read a question and provided the number of answers to the question, which was always at least seven. Questions included both trivia questions with a number of factual answers (for example, naming the Seven Wonders of the Ancient World), and survey questions in which a chosen number of the most common responses formed the pool of acceptable answers."

http://en.wikipedia.org/wiki/Hot_Potato_%28game_show%29

The following "hot potato" references are from the Urban Dictionary online. http://www.urbandictionary.com/

---"A high-priority work task that top management is waiting for, usually involving the sequential efforts of multiple employees. It will burn anyone who holds onto it too long. Upon being assigned such a task, an employee's goal should be to complete their part and pass it to a colleague as quickly as possible, before suffering the wrath of management. As in 'a hot potato just arrived in my inbox, so I'll have to work late tonight.'" by Linguanalyst March 14, 2012

---"A noun for an attractive person who seemingly can't hold on to the same partner for long (be it because of personality, drugs, psychological issues or overprotective ex-marine father), and because of this gets passed along like a hot potato. 'Man, poor Jenna is such a hot potato. I'd totally tap that though.'"by Sodapops March 02, 2013

---"The verb to "hot potato" someone refers to passing gas in the presence of others and immediately passing the blame on to the closest person with a disgusted gesture or surprised face." Submitted by Dave Fishmesiter June 04, 2007

The Science of Hot Potatoes:
Why hot potatoes are so hot and hold their heat so long.

"It is true that, long after the asparagus has gone cold, your baked potato will be deliciously, or perhaps dangerously warm. The reason behind this is the high heat capacity of a potato. Technically speaking, heat capacity (or "specific heat") is how much heat is needed to change the temperature of a substance by one degree. Potatoes trump asparagus in the density department. With more than twice as much density, an equal serving of potatoes and asparagus would have the potatoes staying warm twice as long. Another important part of your supper's ability to retain heat is conductivity and surface area. The heat from your food gets transferred to the cooler air around it, and the more it is in contact with the air, the faster this transfer can take place. For this reason long skinny french fries will cool much faster than a solidly round baked potato. (A sphere is the best shape for minimal surface area to maximum volume.) So when your asparagus comes out of the oven at the same time as your potatoes, start with the greens to save yourself from a burning mouth."
http://lsned.com/facts/hot-potato/

Hot Baked Potatoes
Idaho is the state that produces the most potatoes. The Idaho baked potato was heavily promoted by the Northern Pacific Railway in the early 20th century, often using Hollywood movie stars. For instance, actress Lillian Russell showed off the difference between the railroad's large potatoes (top) and the common varieties (bottom) in this 1915 promotional postcard.

Lillian Russell and a few of the other Great Big Potatoes
Northern Pacific Dining Car Dept.

The Route of the Great Big Baked Potato

"Hazen Titus was appointed as the railway's dining car superintendent in 1908. He talked to Yakima Valley farmers who complained that they were unable to sell their potato crops because their potatoes were simply too large. They fed them to hogs. Titus learned that a single potato could weigh from two to five pounds, but that smaller potatoes were preferred by the end buyers of the vegetable and that many considered them not to be edible because they were difficult to cook because of their thick, rough skin.

"Titus and his staff discovered the "inedible" potatoes were delicious after baking in a slow oven. He contracted to purchase as many potatoes as the farmers could produce that were more than two pounds in weight. Soon after the first delivery of "Netted Gem Bakers," they were offered to diners on the North Coast Limited beginning in 1909. Word of the line's specialty offering traveled quickly, and before long it was using "The Great Big Baked Potato" as a slogan to promote the railroad's passenger service. When an addition was built for the Northern Pacific's Seattle commissary in 1914, a reporter wrote, "A large trademark, in the shape of a baked potato, 40 ft.long and 18 ft. in diameter, surmounts the roof. The potato is electric lighted and its eyes, through the electric mechanism, are made to wink constantly. A cube of butter thrust into its split top glows intermittently." Premiums such as postcards, letter openers, and spoons were also produced to promote "The Route of the Great Big Baked Potato." This slogan served the Northern Pacific for about 50 years. The song "Great Big Baked Potato" (words by N.R. Streeter and H. Caldwell; Music by Oliver George) was written about this potato." http://en.wikipedia.org/wiki/Baked_potato#Idaho

"A baked potato is sometimes called a jacket potato in the United Kingdom. The baked potato has been popular in the UK for many years. In the mid-19th century, jacket potatoes were sold on the streets by hawkers during the autumn and winter months. In London, it was estimated that some 10 tons of baked potatoes were sold each day by this method. Common jacket potato fillings (or "toppings") in the United Kingdom include cheese and beans, tuna mayonnaise, chili con carne and chicken and bacon. Baked potatoes are often eaten on Guy Fawkes Night; traditionally they were often baked in the glowing embers of a bonfire." http://en.wikipedia.org/wiki/Baked_potato#United_Kingdom

An Australian non-profit uses actual hot potatoes to call attention to an on-going "hot potato" issue of how asylum seekers are treated, Down Under. The group serves baked potatoes from a van that is plastered with information about the plight of refugees. "The asylum seeker issue has been an Australian political hot potato for as long as we can remember. Passed from one politician to another, who seem to manipulate the facts to score points, and not actually solve the problem. That's why we created the hot potato van. And on the eve of the general election, we took it on the road. Visiting ten towns over ten days, busting ten myths, serving 10,000 potatoes, inspiring ten million conversations." http:// thehotpotato.com.au/

The Ever-Popular Hot Potato Games and Toys

"How To Play Hot Potato" The object is to keep the ball moving, and out of your hands. If the music stops and it's in your hands, you're out! Requires at least four people, but more people make for more fun. Players arrange themselves in a circle and toss a small, round object (a tennis ball, an orange, or even a real potato will suffice) to each other while music plays. The player who is holding the "hot potato" when the music stops is out. The game continues until one player is left. That player is the winner."

"Through this playful game, young children are able to hone their hand-eye coordination as well as their motor skills. Above all, laughter is the goal. Put a simple twist on the rules: anyone who drops the "hot potato" is also out." by Zachary Collinger http://www.grandparents.com/grandkids/activities-games-and-crafts/hot-potato

Here's a more grown-up version of the same game. Taking turns, one person names a category, for instance, "presidents from west of the Appalachian Mountains" or "hot potato issues of the 19th century," "foreign policy hot potatoes," or "presidents named James or John." The starter then calls out something that fits that category while passing the "hot potato" to the next person who must juggle it while thinking of something that fits the category and so forth. The popular playground game "Four Square" is really a variation of "Hot Potato." Instead of passing the potato, Four Square players bounce (and sometimes toss) a ball.

Hot Potato! Educational Game for 5 to 7 year olds

"This activity is to help students grasp the idea of consonant blends, such as sh, th, or bl. After reviewing the sounds of specified blends, we form a circle and play a "hot potato" type game (I use a bean bag). The leader says a word which starts with a blend, i.e. "small," then tosses the bean bag to another child, who has to say a word that starts with the same blend as "small". That child then tosses to another child and can say "change it." The child who gets the bean bag has to come up with a new blend, and continues as before." This activity can be used for many teaching concepts under review.
http://www.teachingideas.co.uk/english/hotpotato.htm

Hot Potato Games and Toys

"Oh, the drama of a good Hot Potato game: "Quick, man, don't dilly-dally! That potato is scalding your hands even as we speak! Throw it! Throw it!!" The mounting pressure—knowing that the music was about to stop, the timer was about to ding, etc.—made Hot Potato more than a game, but a matter of life or death (kind of like "Don't step in the molten lava," but with more formal rules).

"Nobody knows when the first proto-Hot-Potato game was played (possibly by 18th-century Irish kids with real scalding potatoes—we're just guessing), but by the 1950s, manufactured Hot Potato games were already on store shelves. This was a game that even the very young could understand: A group of kids stood in a circle, somebody played some music or whistled a tune, and the potato got passed around as quickly as possible. Whoever ended up with the potato when the music stopped was kicked out, and the potato elimination match continued.

"To encourage parents to shell out cash for a game they could actually play for free (plus the cost of a single potato), inventive toy manufacturers dreamed up ways to make their own versions of Hot Potato unique and irresistible. Remco's late 50's version used small plastic pans for each player, covered up so that the loser-to-be wouldn't be revealed until the proper time. The majority of Hot Potato sets, however, went the more traditional route. The potato itself was passed around the group, but here's the kicker: this was no ordinary potato.

"In the 1960s, there was "Spudsie," a cute little fellow who had to be wound up before every game. When the wound-up power wound down, Spudsie gave off a "DING," metaphorically torching the hands of one unlucky player. The 1980s brought battery-powered "Chip O'Grattin," along with a slight play alteration. Getting stuck with the potato meant drawing a card with a letter on it. Once a player spelled H-O-T, he or she was out of luck and out of the game. The most recent Hot Potato is a battery-powered talker who shouts out a jubilant "Yahoo!" when his timer's up (sure, he's happy, he's not the one left holding a volcanic spud.)

"Hot Potato remains a must-play at preschool parties, teaching kids hand-eye coordination, catching skills, and the valuable lesson that hot things should quickly be given to somebody else."
http://www.skooldays.com/categories/toys/ty1026.htm

Here's more about hot potato-themed toys and games.

"Jim Prentice Electric Potato Game" from the Electric Company of Holyoke, Massachusetts was a battery operated board game from the 1930s.

"Spudsie, the Hot Potato Game" was produced by Ohio Art in the 1960s. To play the game, wind Spudsie up and toss him around until his timer goes off. The player left holding the potato is "out." The hard red plastic version with a wind up feature was replaced with a stuffed fabric tater.

"Hot Potato: The Musical Potato Action Game" from Parker Brothers had a battery-free stuffed fabric hot potato known as "Chip O'Grattin" that only needed a squeeze to start him playing "Pop Goes the Weasel."

Here are some 21st century hot potato-themed toys: "Daron Shock Ball" Hot Potato Game; "Bouncing Tigger Hot Potato Game" from Disney; "Mr. Potato Head Electronic Talking Plush Doll Game" from Hasbro and "Lumpy the Coal" Holiday Hot Potato Game Ornament from Hallmark (plays Jingle Bells.)

See pictures and descriptions of hot potato toys and games, vintage and new, at Ebay.com.

Hot Potato Challenges

---Rank the hot potatoes from each administration from hardest to easiest to handle.
---Make a list of the top ten hottest potatoes of all time.
---Take turns with friends picking a hot potato from the two lists and see who can write down the cleverest headline.
---Take turns tossing our hot potatoes (or pardons, see list below) from the list and see who can name the appropriate president.

Two "Hot Potato" Quizzes

Presidential pardons have created "hot potatoes" for every chief executive. "Approximately 20,000 pardons and clemencies were issued by U.S. presidents in the 20th century alone. As granted by the Constitution (Article II, Section 2, Clause 1), Presidents have the power to grant clemency in one or more of the following ways: the ability to grant a full pardon, to commute a sentence, or to rescind a fine. A pardon is an executive order vacating a conviction. A commutation is the mitigation of the sentence of someone currently serving a sentence for a crime pursuant to a conviction, without vacating the conviction itself."http://en.wikipedia.org/wiki/ List_of_people_pardoned_or_granted_clemency_by_the_President_of_th e_United_States

Presidential Pardons "Hot Potatoes" Pop Quiz
(Pardons for each president are in random order. Use these numbers with the answer key that follows.)

01
Pardon of Brigham Young for role in the Utah War; Daniel Vandersmith a former judge, pardoned for forgery
02
Pardons of George R. Dale and Roy Olmstead for violating the National Prohibition Act; Duncan Renaldo arrested for illegal entry into the US; Warren T. McCray, Governor of Indiana convicted of Mail Fraud; Thomas W. Miller conspiring to defraud the U.S. government
03
Pardons of Jimmy Hoffa convicted of fraud and bribery, sentence commuted; Angelo DeCarlo convicted of extortion; William Calley convicted of murder for his involvement in the My Lai Massacre

04

Pardons of James Brooks, Texas Ranger indicted for manslaughter; Rudger Clawson convicted of polygamy; David King Udall convicted on perjury charges

05

Pardon of John C. Fremont, convicted by court martial of mutiny, who later became the 1856 Republican candidate for the Presidency of the United States.

06

Pardon of John Scotchlar, for stealing rigging from the new USS Constitution

07

Pardons of Patty Hearst, Marc Rich, Dan Rostenkowski. Fife Symington III, Susan McDougal, Henry Cisneros, Henry O. Flipper, the first black West Point cadet who was found guilty of "conduct unbecoming an officer" in 1882 and Rick Hendrick, NASCAR team owner and champion; convicted of mail fraud

08

Pardons of Frank W. Boykin, Congressman convicted of bribery; Maurice Hutcheson contempt of Congress

09

Pardons of John Hicklin Hall – role in the Oregon land fraud scandal; Charles W. Morse convicted of violations of federal banking laws; Captain Van Schaick for the General Slocum steamship disaster of 1904

10

Pardons of Servillano Aquino convicted for anti-American activities in the Philippines; Al Jennings – sentenced to life in prison for robbery; Stephen A. Douglas Puter convicted of land fraud

11

Pardons of Confederate leaders following the Amnesty Act of 1872

12

Pardon of David Brown convicted of sedition under the Sedition Act of 1798 because of his criticism of the United States federal government

13

Pardon of Ezra Heywood convicted of violating the 1873 Comstock Act

14

Pardons of individuals convicted of various drug and liquor law violations; James Bernard Banks, of Liberty, Utah, illegal possession of government property; Laurens Dorsey, of Syracuse, N.Y., for conspiracy to defraud by making false statements to the Food and Drug Administration

15

Pardons of 264 of 303 Dakota Indians who attacked white settlers in the Great Sioux Uprising of 1862; Clement Vallandigham - Copperhead sentenced for disloyalty; sentence commuted, and deported to the Confederacy; various men who enlisted in the army, but who among other circumstances were underage, bounty jumpers, or AWOL

16

Pardons of George Burdick, a New York newspaper editor, who had refused to testify in federal court regarding the sources used in his article concerning the collection of customs duties; Frederick Krafft convicted for alleged violation of the Espionage Act

17

Commutations of Marcus Garvey, convicted of mail fraud, later deported; Lothar Witzke a German spy and saboteur, deported

18

Pardons of George Caldwell convicted for income tax evasion; James Michael Curley and Richard W. Leche convicted for mail fraud; Andrew J. May convicted for accepting bribes; Seymour Weiss convicted for tax evasion and mail fraud;

Oscar Collazo for attempted Truman assassination. Death sentence was commuted to life in prison

19

Commutations for Lewis "Scooter" Libby, assistant to President George W. Bush and Chief of Staff to Dick Cheney , who was convicted of perjury in connection with the CIA leak scandal involving members of the State Department who 'outed' CIA agent Valerie Plame; José Compeán and Ignacio Ramos, two U.S. Border Patrol agents who wounded drug smuggler Osvaldo Aldrete Dávila and tried to cover up the incident; John Forté, hip-hop singer and song writer convicted for smuggling cocaine

20

Pardon of Warren T. McCray, governor of Indiana, convicted of mail fraud and Thomas W. Miller, defrauding the U.S. government

21

Pardon of Philip Vigol (or Wigle) and John Mitchell, convicted of treason in the Whiskey Rebellion

22

Pardons of W. Mark Felt and Edward S. Miller, FBI officials, convicted of authorizing illegal break-ins. Mark Felt later in life admitted to being Deep Throat, the informant during the Watergate affair; Junior Johnson convicted of moonshining; George Steinbrenner; Marvin Mandel

23

Pardons of Richard Nixon, granted a full and unconditional pardon just before he could be indicted; Robert E. Lee, the Confederate general's full rights of citizenship were posthumously restored; Iva Toguri D'Aquino known as "Tokyo Rose," the only U.S. citizen convicted of treason; conditional amnesty to over 50,000 draft dodgers

24

Pardon of "Billy Wilson" (David L. Anderson) convicted outlaw

25

Unconditional amnesty to all Confederates; earlier amnesties requiring signed oaths and excluding certain classes of people were issued to Alexander H. Stephens, Vice President of the Confederate States of America, Samuel Arnold, Dr. Samuel Mudd and Edmund Spangler, charged with conspiring to murder Lincoln

26

Commutations for Eugene V. Debs and Kate Richards O'Hare both convicted of sedition under the Espionage Act of 1917

27

Pardons for men involved in the Iran-Contra Affair; Myra Soble conviction for her involvement in the Rosenberg spy ring; commutation for Joseph Occhipinti, Federal drug agent convicted of violation of civil rights, perjury and depravation of rights

28

Pardons of first-time offenders convicted of crimes under the Narcotics Control Act of 1956 overturning much of the law passed by Congress

29

Pardon of G. Gordon Liddy convicted for his role in Watergate; Vietnam draft dodgers were given unconditional amnesty issued in the form of a pardon; Jefferson Davis, President of the Confederate States of America

30

Commutation of Maurice L. Schick convicted in a military court-martial for brutal murder; death sentence commuted to life imprisonment, with the condition that he would never be released; legal challenge went to the Supreme Court, questioning the constitutionality of the punishment "Life Imprisonment Without Parole;" decided in Schick v. Reed that to be so sentenced was constitutional

31

Pardons of Alexander McKenzie who was held in contempt of court; Charles Chilton Moore who was jailed for blasphemy

32

Pardons to members of The Church of Jesus Christ of Latter-day Saints for the offense of engaging in polygamous or plural marriage

33

Commutation for Fitz John Porter who was court-martialed for his actions at Second Bull Run

34

Pardons of Daniel Drayton and Edward Sayres convicted in the "Pearl Incident" transporting slaves to freedom

35

Pardon for Alexander William Holmes, a sailor convicted of voluntary manslaughter

36

Pardons of William Hull, former Governor of the Michigan Territory, sentenced to death for surrendering Fort Detroit; Jean Lafitte, Pierre Lafitte and others for piracy, granted due to their assistance during the War of 1812

37

Pardons for numerous individuals convicted of piracy

38

Pardoned, commuted or rescinded the convictions of 386 people, among them George Wilson, convicted of robbing the United States mail. He later refused to accept the pardon.

39

Pardon for William Lyon Mackenzie, convicted for violation of American neutrality laws

40

Pardons for Captain L. O. Helland arrested for having more passengers on board a vessel than were allowed by American law; Wekau and Chickhonsic who were Ho-Chunk leaders pardoned for their role in the Winnebago War

Can you name the four presidents who issued no pardons or commutations?

<u>Presidential Pardons Pop Quiz Answers</u>

1 Buchanan; 2 F. Roosevelt; 3 Nixon; 4 Cleveland's 1st term; 5 Polk; 6 J. Adams; 7 Clinton; 8 L. Johnson; 9 Taft; 10 T. Roosevelt; 11 Grant; 12 Jefferson; 13 Hayes; 14 Obama; 15 Lincoln; 16 Wilson; 17 Coolidge; 18 Truman; 19 GW Bush; 20 Hoover; 21 Washington; 22 Reagan; 23 Ford; 24 Cleveland's 2nd term; 25 A. Johnson; 26 Harding; 27 GHW Bush; 28 Kennedy; 29 Carter; 30 Eisenhower; 31 McKinley; 32 B. Harrison; 33 Arthur; 34 Fillmore; 35 Tyler; 36 Madison; 37 Monroe; 38 Jackson; 39 Van Buren; 40 JQ Adams

W. Harrison, Taylor, Pierce and Garfield didn't issue any pardons or commutations.

<u>Category: "Presidents and Potatoes"</u>
(featuring as many potato references as could be dug up)

01 He got a heart-shaped potato while on a trip to the Big Apple.

02 His favorite election night meal was steak, baked potato and butter pecan ice cream. Change one letter of this president's name to identify the subject of this quiz.

03 Growing up he sometimes only had potatoes to eat, and later christened a town named after him with watermelon juice.

04 This president grew up in Europe, regularly eating potato-laden Russian and Dutch meals.

05 His personally selected French chef prepared 21 course state dinners featuring the finest of potato dishes.

06 The president who was the first to have French fries served at the White House.

07 As a senator he broke with the Democratic Party to support the Homestead Act which provided 160 acres to farmers who worked the land for five years. Frequently the first crop planted was potatoes.

08 Which president had a great-grandpa who escaped pirates who took over his fishing boat and a father who was a farming failure?

09 This president frequently stopped at fast food places for burgers and fries on his daily run.

10 Which president grew up on a farm and later managed it for ten years? During a campaign stop in Idaho, he told the audience about a time he was on a military inspection tour to Maine and encountered an Idaho soldier who was being held in the guardhouse for refusing to peel Maine potatoes while on KP duty.

11 Before he became president, he organized famine relief for the Belgian people, shipping potatoes and other rations to Europe.

12 This president is better known for peanuts than potatoes.

13 As a boy he picked beans part time and as president made a historic trip to the planet's largest potato-producing nation.

14 This former Ohio farm boy's presidency was marred by a teapot.

15 As a boy he worked in the family potato patch and later was a cattle rancher.

16 His childhood meals heavily featured potatoes. He famously said, "an army fights best on a full stomach," and was a creative battlefield cook.

17 This president preferred potatoes to broccoli.

18 At 340 pounds and a BMI of 42.3 he was the most overweight president who once wrote "no real gentleman weighs more than 300 pounds." He shed 60 of them on a low carb and sugar diet.

19 He could write *solanum tuberosum*, (Latin for the potato,) with one hand while simultaneously writing "potato" in Greek with the other.

20 He warned European powers to stay away from the homeland of the potato and other Latin American nations.

21 His ancestors came from an Irish village which means "place of the small potatoes." He enjoyed telling a joke about potatoes in the Soviet Union.

22 As a soldier in the Civil War, this president delivered potatoes and other rations through heavy enemy fire.

23 Who caught pneumonia while out at a DC market buying potatoes and other provisions?

24 Whose wife did not serve alcoholic drinks in the White House and was known as Lemonade Lucy?

25 Upon retiring from the Army, he raised potatoes on a Missouri farm before being elected president.

26 This president grew potatoes, produced maple syrup and operated a cheese factory.

27 Nicknamed "doughface" by his detractors, he owned a Pennsylvania estate called "Wheatland."

28 His home was a working farm on Long Island, at the time a leading producer of potatoes.

29 This president's ancestors came to America as a result of the Irish Potato Famine. His onetime actress girlfriend's career took off when she posed for a publicity photo wearing a potato sack dress.

30 During whose presidency did Commodore Perry's gifts to Japan include a barrel of potatoes?

31 He said, "The man who reads everything is like the man who eats everything: he can digest nothing."

32 His wife first served ice cream at the White House.

33 Among many crops, he grew potatoes on his farm but was the only president of the first five not to own a plantation.

34 Which former Kentucky farmer and Louisiana plantation owner may have died from food poisoning?

35 His White House cook over-boiled everything and yet this president never fired her.

36 He fathered fifteen little potato eaters, more than any other president, and retired to his Walnut Grove plantation in Virginia.

37 Which president was a cabbage and potato farmer in New York?

38 This president was born and raised on a farm in North Bend, Ohio, the same state where an annual potato festival is held and a record-setting pile of mashed potatoes was prepared.

39 He provided a huge wheel of cheese for the public attending his inauguration reception. He later held elaborate dinner parties in his highly decorative dining room.

40 He owned a farm in the state where the first commercial potato crop in the nation was grown.

41 During whose administration did the Department of Agriculture become an executive agency?

42 "Martin's" was the preferred potato chip served on board his Air Force One flights.

43 The only president born in the Garden State, "Uncle Jumbo," loved to eat, hated exercise and consequently struggled with his weight all his life. At 240-280 pounds and a BMI 34.6, he was the second most overweight president. At 18, doctors put him on a three day "starvation diet."

44 Around his birthday is the traditional time to plant potatoes. A favorite meal was strips of steak and potato baked together.

Category: "Presidents and Potatoes" answers

1 Obama, 2 Ford, 3 Lincoln, 4 JQ Adams, 5 Arthur, 6 Jefferson, 7 A Johnson, 8 Fillmore, 9 Clinton, 10 Truman, 11 Hoover, 12 Carter, 13 Nixon, 14 Harding, 15 L Johnson 16 Eisenhower, 17 GHW Bush, 18 Taft, 19 Garfield, 20 Monroe, 21 Reagan, 22 McKinley, 23 W Harrison, 24 Hayes, 25 Grant, 26 Coolidge, 27 Buchanan, 28 T Roosevelt, 29 Kennedy, 30 Polk, 31 Wilson, 32 Madison, 33 J Adams, 34 Taylor, 35 F Roosevelt, 36 Tyler, 37 Van Buren, 38 B Harrison, 39 Jackson, 40 Pierce, 41 Cleveland's first, 42 GW Bush, 43 Cleveland's second, 44 Washington

Notes
Potatoes came from the Americas and were a staple in the early years of independence. An anthology of presidential recipes, *The President's Cookbook,* edited by Poppy Cannon and Patricia Brooks, describes a favorite recipe of Martha Washington for "stoved" potatoes, baked slowly in the oven, layered with beef steaks.

"According to food historian Karen Hess, it's also possible that Jefferson initiated America's love affair with French fries. Long before American soldiers encountered them in Europe during World War I, Jefferson reportedly served the addictive fare while entertaining guests at the President's House. Having hired a maître d'hôtel and chef from France to manage provisions and food preparations, Jefferson and his guests likely benefitted from an imported knowledge of deep-fried slices of potatoes." (http://www.history.com/news/hungry-history/thomas-jefferson-americas-pioneering-gourmand)

"When Ulysses S. Grant resigned from the military in 1854, he longed to spend time with his wife Julia and their young children. Since the army no longer provided him an income, he planned to support his family by farming at White Haven. Cultivating the 80 acres given to the Grants as a wedding gift, Ulysses also managed the rest of the land of his father-in-law, Colonel Frederick Dent. With the help of the Dents' slaves, Grant planted crops of potatoes and wheat, corded wood, harvested fruit from the orchards, and tended a vegetable garden. He was so dedicated to this future that he commented to a friend, "whoever hears of me in ten years will hear of a well-to-do old Missouri farmer." (http://www.nps.gov/ulsg/learn/historyculture/hardscrabble.htm)

"For a President in the Big Apple, a Heart-Shaped Potato"
"President Obama's first stop was at the Ed Sullivan Theater on Broadway to tape his first appearance on the Letterman show since being elected. A woman from Missouri brought a heart-shaped potato to the show's taping, and Mr. Letterman did a Top 10 list of reasons Mr. Obama agreed to do the show (No. 6: "Someone offers you 600 bucks, you take it, ladies and gentlemen"). Mr. Obama's own explanation: "The main reason I'm here? I want to see that heart-shaped potato." The woman tossed the potato to Mr. Letterman, who gave it to the president, who put it in his pocket. 'This is remarkable,' he said."
by Helene Cooper for *The New York Times*, 9/21/09

President Reagan delighted in collecting and telling jokes about the Soviet Union. Here's one of his favorites. A Soviet official visiting a state-owned potato farm asks a farmer how things are going, and the farmer replies that the harvest is so bountiful that the potatoes would reach the "foot of God" if piled on top of one another. "But this is the Soviet Union," says the commissar, "there is no God here." The farmer replies, "That's all right, there are no potatoes, either."
http://www.nytimes.com/1987/08/21/us/washington-talk-reagan-and-the-russians-the-joke-s-on-them.html

Memorize the Presidents: Three by Three

Washington Adams Jefferson
Madison Monroe Adams
Jackson Van Buren Harrison
Tyler Polk Taylor
Fillmore Pierce Buchanan
Lincoln Johnson Grant
Hayes Garfield Arthur
Cleveland Harrison Cleveland
McKinley Roosevelt Taft
Wilson Harding Coolidge
Hoover Roosevelt Truman
Eisenhower Kennedy Johnson
Nixon Ford Carter
Reagan Bush Clinton
Bush Obama

By diminutive nicknames:

Georgie, Johnny, Tommy
Jimmy, Jimmy, Johnny
Andy, Marty, Billy
Johnny, Jimmy, Zack
Fill, Franky, Jimmy
Abe, Andy, U
Ruthy, Jimmy, Chessy
Grovey, Benny, Grovey
Billy, Teddy, Billy
Woody, Winnie, Cal
Herb, Franky, Harry
Ike, Johnny, Lyn
Dicky, Gerry, Jimmy
Ronny, Georgie, Billy
Georgie, Barry

List of presidential nicknames from "Father of his country" to "No Drama Obama."

h t t p : / / e n . w i k i p e d i a . o r g / w i k i / List_of_nicknames_of_United_States_Presidents

Here's another list with nicknames explained.

http://mentalfloss.com/article/57009/30-presidential-nicknames-explained

Ten tough presidential decisions

http://blog.constitutioncenter.org/2011/08/office-politics-10-tough-presidential-decisions/

Nicknames Matter

"In 2005 the consultancy Tagline Guru conducted a small survey of professionals in the fields of branding, marketing, and advertising aimed at identifying the "best" U.S. city slogans and nicknames. Participants were asked to evaluate about 800 nicknames and 400 slogans, considering several criteria in their assessments. The assigned criteria were: whether the nickname or slogan expresses the "brand character, affinity, style, and personality" of the city, whether it "tells a story in a clever, fun, and memorable way," uniqueness and originality, and whether it "inspires you to visit there, live there, or learn more."

The top-ranked nickname in the survey was New York City's "The Big Apple," followed by "Sin City" (Las Vegas), "The Big Easy" (New Orleans), "Motor City" (Detroit), and "The Windy City" (Chicago). In addition to the number-two nickname, Las Vegas had the top-rated slogan: "What Happens Here, Stays Here." The second- through fifth-place slogans were "So Very Virginia" (Charlottesville, Virginia), "Always Turned On" (Atlantic City, New Jersey), "Cleveland Rocks!" (Cleveland, Ohio), and "The Sweetest Place on Earth"(Hershey, Pennsylvania.) http://en.wikipedia.org/wiki/List_of_city_nicknames_in_the_United_States

As far as nicknames go, Washington's current "It's a Capital City" beats "The Cherry Pit Spitting Capital of the World: Eau Claire, MI and Gallup, New Mexico's "Drunk Driving Capital of America" or "Poison Oak Capital of the World: Forestville, CA," for sure. But still WDC's nickname can and should be much punchier.

Washington, DC "The Hot Potato." We can do this.

Our mission is clear. And then the next goal will be to have Washington's "The Hot Potato" acclaimed the world's best city nickname. Do it for old DC.

Author's Notes

As a former resident of DC, within sight of Eastern Market on Capitol Hill, I still return annually if not more often. I love and admire the city's people, parks, gardens, museums, historic landmarks, alleys, traditions, transit systems, and even the weather. As a life long geography nerd, map hugger and student of place nicknames, slogans and mottos, I am determined to help WDC get properly nicknamed.

That kind of determination, although I can't prove it, certainly helped nudge C-Span into geographical accuracy. Now they properly identify members of Congress by key locations in their districts and not solely by their states, which only Senators represent. Many times I called into C-Span programs, when appropriate, and delivered my pitch as often as I could get through. My son was one of the national winners of C-Span's American Presidents contest and my wife and I accompanied him to Washington, DC. There I seized the opportunity during a reception for the winners to discuss my issue with C-Span's executives. Eventually, without any fanfare, C-Span began more precisely identifying all members of Congress. For instance, my current Congressman went from being identified on screen as Ben Ray Luhan, D-NM to Ben Ray Luhan, D-New Mexico, 3rd District (Santa Fe, Gallup, Las Vegas, Taos.)

Yes, I started the world's first museum about the potato with my students at The International School of Brussels in Belgium. Yes, the collection is said to be the world's largest on the history and social influence of the potato. It's been featured in the Smithsonian's Seeds of Change exhibition, as well as at The National Museum of Science and Technology in Ottawa, Canada. Most recently, my wife and I organized an exhibition called "Spuds Unearthed!" which was on display at the U.S. Botanic Garden in DC for five months. And yes,

The Potato Museum is still in search of a permanent home. And, after thirty years, I still believe "The Hot Potato" is the perfect nickname for WDC.

Developing this DC nickname campaign, I've enjoyed the unique refresher course it has offered in American political history. Studying politics and decision-making with this "hot potato" focus can be a rewarding, fun and memorable way to engage students. In addition, this "hot potato approach" helps focus in on key themes for each era of our nation's history. It says a lot that certain of the hottest taters have been passed along for decades and many succeeding administrations before being settled. Immigration and health care reform now; tariffs and civil service reform then.

Born in Philadelphia and raised in the historic Quaker community of Haddonfield in Southern New Jersey, I have degrees from Syracuse University and City College of New York. I met my future wife, Meredith Sayles, while we were both studying in Florence, Italy. We later married in Tehran, Iran where we were teaching with the U.S. Peace Corps. For a decade we worked in Brussels, Belgium and traveled extensively throughout Europe. My initial interest in food history was sparked while teaching fifth grade at the International School of Brussels when I started The Potato Museum with my students.

Now Meredith and I have created "The Food Museum Online" http://www.foodmuseum.com and "The Global Food Heritage Project."

Visit EATS Publishing for more information on my food-related books. (https://www.facebook.com/eatspublishing)

Food Heritage Matters: Preserving Personal, Local, Global Histories and Sites, 2015

Eats Pinellas: Food History and Heritage Sites Tour, 2015

Eats Haddonfield: a tour of food heritage sites, 2014

Gastronomie: Food Museums and Heritage Sites of France, 2005, co-authored with, but really written by Meredith Sayles Hughes (Bunker Hill Publishing)

Meredith and Tom Hughes at The Potato Museum's "Spuds Unearthed!" exhibition, a collaboration with the US Botanic Garden in 2010.

Just some of my International School of Brussels students in
the 1970s who were there at the beginning of
The Potato Museum.
We stay connected on Facebook.
https://www.facebook.com/pages/The-Potato-Museum/
111742613406?ref=hl

Still a Hot Potato

Official prayers for Obama are a political hot potato

Look out! Keystone XL Pipeline Project Hot Potato Incoming

Republicans are playing hot potato with Homeland Security funding

Dropping a Client Like a "Hot Potato"

U.S. Supreme Court Passes the Buck on Affirmative Action Hot Potato

Obama and Congress Play Hot Potato With War Powers in Syria

High Court Ducks Hot Potato Case

Senate tosses shutdown hot potato back to House

HOT POTATO BENGHAZI

"Still a Hot Potato" http://culberthealth.com/blog/?p=602

"Official prayers for Obama are a political hot potato" http://www.usatoday.com/story/news/politics/2013/01/17/obama-prayer-inauguration-cathedral/1842775/

"Look out! Keystone XL Pipeline Project Hot Potato Incoming" http://grassrootsne.com/the-new-national-past-time-pipeline-hot-potato/

"Republicans are playing hot potato with Homeland Security Funding" http://www.washingtonpost.com/opinions/the-gop-plays-hot-potato-with-dhs-funding/2015/02/16/1a94aed8-b3d0-11e4-886b-c22184f27c35_story.html

"Dropping a client like a hot potato" http://dqed.com/2014/11/23/dropping-a-client-like-a-hot-potato/

"U.S. Supreme Court Passes the Buck on Affirmative Action Hot Potato" http://www.sunshinestatenews.com/story/us-supreme-court-passes-buck-affirmative-action-hot-potato

"Obama and Congress Play Hot Potato with War Powers in Syria" http://time.com/3198292/barack-obama-syria-iraq-isis-congress/

"High Court Ducks Hot Potato Case" http://www.cbsnews.com/news/high-court-ducks-hot-potato-case/

"Senate tosses shutdown hot potato back to House" http://www.cnn.com/2013/09/27/politics/shutdown-showdown/

"Hot Potato Benghazi" http://soopermexican.com/2012/11/02/obama-hillary-and-panetta-play-hot-potato-benghazi/

www.ingramcontent.com/pod-product-compliance
Lightning Source LLC
Chambersburg PA
CBHW070812290526
45795CB00002B/698